UNDERSTANDING COMPASSION

Martina E. Faulkner MSW

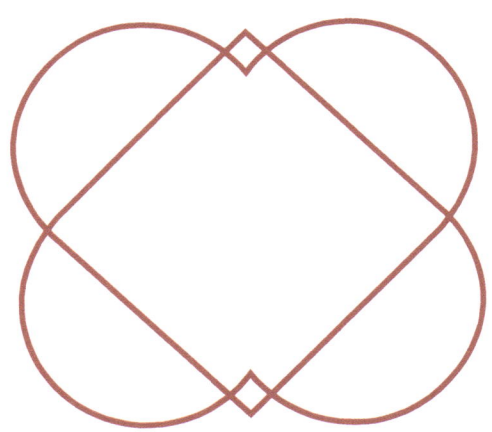

INSPIREBYTES OMNI MEDIA

Understanding Compassion

Copyright © 2025 Martina E. Faulkner

This publication is published and distributed worldwide in the English language in the following formats:

ISBN Paperback: 978-1-969348-02-0
ISBN E-Book: 978-1-969348-03-7

This book was printed in a manner that minimizes its impact on the planet and the environment. Learn more at: www.inspirebytes.com/why-we-publish-differently/

INSPIREBYTES OMNI MEDIA

Inspirebytes Omni Media LLC
PO Box 988
Wilmette, IL 60091

For more information, please visit www.inspirebytes.com
Graphics and photos: Canva Design Pro

"Love and compassion are necessities, not luxuries. Without them humanity cannot survive."

– Dalai Lama –

"Our human compassion binds us the one to the other - not in pity or patronizingly, but as human beings who have learnt how to turn our common suffering into hope for the future."

– Nelson Mandela –

"The purpose of human life is to serve, and to show compassion and the will to help others."

– Albert Schweitzer –

Contents

"The dew of compassion is a tear."

— Lord Byron —

Introduction

Compassion is a topic that can feel incredibly subjective, though the ample research implies some measure of objectivity. In the early 2000s, Dr. Kristin Neff pioneered the first empirical studies of self-compassion after becoming interested in the practice alongside Buddhism. Considered the foremost authority on the subject, Dr. Neff's work subsequently prompted thousands of studies by other researchers. This volume of research suggests that self-compassion is both measurable (quantifiable) and tangible (qualitative). But self-compassion is a type of compassion, or a directed expression of compassion; so, what is compassion?

The Oxford English Dictionary cites the first use of the word "compassion" in 1340, as: "Suffering together with another, participation in suffering; fellow-feeling, sympathy." Though this definition is currently considered obsolete, the notion of "fellow-feeling" is still an integral piece of the puzzle.

Colloquially, the word "compassion" has evolved to imply a measure of separated concern, such as pity. (e.g. "Have pity on them; show some compassion.") While this may be true, it's not the whole story. In order to truly understand compassion, we must also understand its various components, most of which involve some measure of fellow-feeling. These include: sympathy, empathy, care, and perspective.

For compassion is not just one thing; it's an interplay between various components in a way that engenders both thought and feeling in a way that is greater than the sum of its parts.

What is Compassion?

"Tolerance and compassion are qualities of fearless people."

— Paulo Coelho —

When we talk about compassion, we need to first understand both the players and the components. Unlike self-compassion, when we are discussing compassion, we need to have more than one person or entity involved. Its very nature is dependent on there being at least two players, hence the "fellow-feeling" aspect of compassion still remaining true to this day.

The Players

In any given situation where there is compassion, there are always at least two groups or entities involved. For ease of understanding, we will call these the Giver and the Receiver. Both the Giver and the Receiver can be individuals or groups, in any combination.

The Giver is the person or group that feels concern, care, and/or pity for the Receiver. This can be as a result of a situation or circumstance, or a long-standing hierarchy (noblesse oblige, for example). What it requires is that the Giver express an emotion toward the Receiver in a way that implies either sympathy or empathy (more on the difference between the two in a moment). That emotion can then prompt action, or not. Contrary to common belief, compassion does not always lead to a change in behavior, though it often can.

The Receiver is, therefore, the recipient of the Giver's attention and focus. Sometimes, they benefit from the Giver's awareness and compassion, sometimes they don't. The benefit can be lasting or temporary, based on the situation, and often involves some measure of gratitude on the part of the Receiver, though it is not usually a requirement for receipt.

For example, an unhoused person sitting on a city sidewalk with an open cup may receive money from passers-by as an expression of compassion. While they may respond with a gentle nod or "thank you," it is not a requirement for the gift of charity. Similarly, an entire community that receives a new water well and pump from a charitable organization may feel gratitude toward the group, but may not necessarily express that gratitude directly to the donors to the organization. Nor is the expression of gratitude a requirement of the donation.

Another good example of this is when the Receiver is a living being, but not a human being. In this scenario, the Giver focuses their attention on charitable organizations that support the welfare of animals or environments. Though they may be thanked for their gift of time or resources, the ultimate recipients (i.e. the animals) may not even be aware of the Givers' existence.

More often than not, an expression of compassion is made freely by a Giver, without any expectation of return from the Receiver. In all of these scenarios, there are always two players when it comes to compassion. So, what are the components involved?

> "In order to have
> understanding,
> you need forgiveness,
> compassion, and empathy."
>
> — Rooney Mara —

The Components

As previously mentioned, there are primary components that work together to create what we call compassion. The four most important ones are: Perspective, Sympathy, Empathy, and Care.

These four components are not mutually exclusive and can occur in any combination often with other emotions or experience, which is partially what makes compassion so subjective. It's also why if you ask people to define "compassion," you usually get multiple answers with various qualifiers. If you break it down, however, those answers probably all revolve around some aspect of these four primary components.

Of the four, it's fair to say that there is one that stands above the rest as a requirement for compassion. You may be inclined to think it's "care," but the truth is, it's perspective. Or, more accurately, it's the ability—and desire—to take perspective. This is true even if the Giver isn't consciously aware that they are doing so.

As such, in order to truly understand compassion, we need to start with understanding what it means to "take perspective."

Taking Perspective

The ability to take perspective is a superpower. Full stop. It is one of the most important skills you can acquire in life and possibly the most important tool in your emotional toolbox. If there were a manual for how to succeed at life and be a good human being, it would be listed in the first three steps; it's that important.

Unfortunately, it's not often talked about in this way, and it can sometimes even be disparaged (most often when it is misunderstood and thought of as a weakness). But, if you study the behavior of individuals with high emotional intelligence, it's likely that they all know how to take perspective and probably practice it quite regularly and subconsciously.

Why is it so important, though? What does it do for us, individually, and as a whole?

In order to understand why this is so important, we need to first accept that it is part of human nature to belong to a group. We require connection and a sense of belonging in order to survive, live, and thrive. It's a biological drive that is true for the vast majority of people on the planet.

This need means that we have to be a part of something, not apart from something.

If we are left out of the group, we risk dying. It's that simple. Even though we are no longer "hunter-gatherers" in our daily life, meaning we no longer need to rely on the group to eat or survive, we are still hard-wired to belong.

And, what makes it easier to belong? The ability to take perspective.

It is an evolutionary skill that has allowed us to make belonging easier. Think about it like this: The last time you underwent some sort of crisis or suffering, it was probably the person who related to you the most that helped you to feel better. They related to you because they could understand your perspective, either from experience or because they have honed their ability to do so.

A Part vs. Apart

These words are often used incorrectly and interchangeably as many assume they are synonyms simply because they sound the same. The truth is they are opposites.

If you are "a part of" something, it means you are connected to it and probably invested in it in some way. For example if you are a part of a team, you want the team to win or succeed at whatever it is doing. You have an interest in seeing things work out. You are a member; you belong.

If, however, you are "apart from" something, it means you are not including yourself in it. Additionally, you are most likely making a statement to make it clear that you are not a part of it and probably not invested in it. You may even have a desire to see things not work out. In other words, it's not something you belong to.

Taking perspective results in an ability to connect, and an ability to connect results in a stronger, healthier group overall. At its core, taking perspective is an evolved survival method. This means that the reverse is also true. Someone who can't take perspective may be unable to connect, which can result in their being ostracized or left on the fringes of the group.

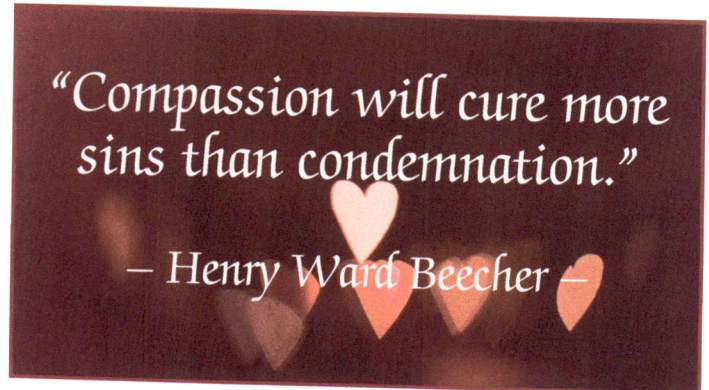

"Compassion will cure more sins than condemnation."

— Henry Ward Beecher —

Their inability to relate has ramifications for them personally and for the larger group, as a whole.

Now, let's take a look at the impact this skill can have on ourselves as well as others, beyond the obvious benefit of connection.

"If we want to create a viable, peaceful world, we've got to integrate compassion into the gritty realities of 21st century life."

— Karen Armstrong —

Perspective and Emotional Evolution

One of the simplest truths about humans is that we are designed to evolve, just like the rest of nature. We are not excused from the biological patterns inherent in being a living being, even though some humans may behave as if they are. Biological evolution, at its core, is a very slow process, often taking generations to show even the smallest shift.

However, there are other forms of evolution that we rarely discuss that humans have somehow managed to hardwire to be faster. Primarily, this includes emotional and mental evolution. The result of mental evolution, which involves the brain and its innovative capacity, is most often seen in technological advances as well as a deeper understanding of concepts and ideas.

Emotional evolution is different. It's also a bit more of a minefield, because true emotional evolution involves some measure of trial and failure in order to build resilience and deepen understanding. Unfortunately, there are many practices and teachings that use "bypassing" in order to achieve the appearance of emotional evolution. When we bypass something, however, we are not learning or evolving; we are simply using a cheat sheet thinking that if we give the "correct" answer to something, we will have evolved. But emotional evolution happens in the learning and practicing, not in the (re)iteration of an answer.

What does this mean when it comes to perspective?

To begin with, the ability to take perspective protects the group. When the group is protected, the individual feels safe. When individuals feel safe they are better able to engage in practices that lead to emotional evolution, both together and alone. This translates to an emotionally evolving group at an exponential pace as the group becomes greater than the sum of its individual parts.

Now, imagine having multiple groups all engaging in emotional evolution in this way. The result is a stronger, more emotionally balanced and healthy society. Move forward some more, and we have stronger communities, countries, and a healthier planet overall.

Why?

Because everyone is able to engage in individual emotional evolution thereby creating pathways for emotional evolution for the whole. Somewhere along the way, even though the initial practice is a solo endeavor, the focus shifts from being me-based to we-based, because people feel supported by one another. That support comes from connection and the connection has its roots in the ability to take perspective.

"Compassion is the ultimate expression of your highest self."

— Russell Simmons —

Taking perspective naturally invites compassion into the conversation—including when taking perspective on your own life. Sometimes, when we feel lost or are struggling, taking a step back to get out of the weeds and get a wider view is the shift we need to see things in a new way and make a different decision. As an added benefit when we do this for others, not only can we see ourselves in their shoes and relate, but we can also help them by accessing that wider view when/if they can't.

Taking perspective involves being able to put yourself into the other's situation. It requires you to set your own experiences, prejudices, and biases aside so that you can access what it might feel like to live as the other, even for the briefest moment. The interplay between the self and the other takes on new meaning when we can see everything and everyone as part of a whole.

Compassion invites us to remember connection, just as connection invites us to be compassionate.

Once we are able to take perspective, a world of options opens up to us when it comes to compassion. These options include the other primary components of compassion: Sympathy, Empathy, and Care.

"Spirituality is allowing compassion and love to flourish. When belongness begins, corruption ends."

— Sri Sri Ravi Shankar —

What Does It Mean To Care?

"We forget some of the oldest medicines we have are love and compassion, and they can be deployed by everyone."

— Vivek Murthy —

Care, simply stated, means to feel concern for. Though there may be variations on this theme, to care for someone or something means you are concerned for it, and most likely for its well-being. You can care for anything (like your home, your garden, or your floors), or anyone (like family, friends, and disenfranchised groups).

Care has no limits to its application, which is why it is a key component of compassion. It also requires two players (unless it's self-care, then it's like self-compassion). However, when it comes to care, the two players do not need to be living beings. That is the main difference between care and compassion. Care can involve inanimate objects, just as it can be focused on the living. However, for the purpose of this discussion on compassion, we will limit ourselves to the care expressed between living beings.

Understanding Compassion

For the most part, we mostly see care as part of relationships. These can be platonic, familial, romantic, or anything that involves at least two people or groups. As a general rule, relationships often involve an unspoken agreement of care.

Of course, there are professional relationships that also involve care, but in those instances, the arrangement is not left unsaid; it's usually written out and negotiated.

For example, a homecare nurse has a specific agreement to provide services in exchange for a fee. Everything will be discussed and negotiated as part of a care agreement

That being said, regardless of the type of relationship (professional or relational), most care-based situations create, or result in, some measure of compassion.

There is a specific type of care, however, that usually requires compassion from the onset: Being a caregiver. Because it's becoming more common as populations live longer, let's take a moment to explore this subcategory of care.

"In separateness lies the world's greatest misery; in compassion lies the world's true strength."

– Buddha –

> *"I don't really think about doing something kind,*
> *I think there's just a way to conduct your daily*
> *life with compassion to other people."*
>
> — Kat Dennings —

As many people around the world are aging, we are seeing a marked increase in the need for at-home caregivers. These can be professionals or volunteers who come into the home to offer support and services, but more often than not, they are family members or relatives. If the latter, the caregiving role often goes beyond the basic premise of "care and concern"—it requires deep compassion.

Caregiving, therefore, is something that sits outside the general definition of caring. In other words, just like care is a necessary component of compassion, compassion is a necessary component of caregiving. In this way, the cause/effect relationship between the two has shifted to one that is more of a "chicken-egg" situation.

Furthermore, when one wanes, it seems to directly (and often negatively) affect the other. They are inextricably intertwined, both needing the other in order to maintain a given situation. While this is the case for most family caregivers, it's especially true for Sideline Caregivers.

Ultimately, care—or caring—is a key component of compassion, mainly because not caring is an expression of disengagement or disinterest. Compassion is an expression of investment, of recognizing that there is something more—that everything ultimately affects everything else in some way. To have compassion is to care.

How you care is up to you, and two of the most common ways are through sympathy and empathy.

What is a Sideline Caregiver?

A Sideline Caregiver is a person who has all (or most) of the responsibility and none (or little) of the agency in caring for another person. Think of a player on the sidelines of any game. Their job is to "participate" in the game by watching every move and play as if they were on the field so that they can be ready to jump in, if needed.

They cannot sit down on the bench and play on their phone, nor can they leave the sideline, just in case they are needed. They are a passive player until they're not, and they don't get to choose when things change.

Many people in the "sandwich generation" are finding themselves becoming Sideline Caregivers while they are still in the process of raising a family. There are probably even more people who are predominantly empty-nesters that are now finding themselves in this new role. And just like an understudy in a play or musical, they have to learn their part (or multiple parts) in order to be ready to take over at a moment's notice, often without warning.

For this group, caring is part of the equation, as is compassion. The reason it might be more exhausting than being a regular caregiver is because of the imbalance between agency and responsibility, as well as the perpetual state of not knowing.

Sideline Caregivers don't know when things will change, they just expect that it will at some point and the balance will shift. In essence, they are waiting for the other proverbial shoe to drop, which may (or may never) happen.

This role, therefore, requires both compassion and self-compassion (often in the form of self-care) for the Sideline Caregiver to try and maintain some semblance of mental, emotional, and physical health.

Sympathy vs. Empathy

"It is above all by the imagination that we achieve perception and compassion and hope."

— Ursula K. Le Guin —

In recent years, much has been discussed around the subject of empathy, mainly due to the viral success of Dr. Brené Brown's TED Talk in 2010: The Power of Vulnerability. In her research, Dr. Brown gave new language to the relationship between vulnerability, courage, empathy, and shame, resulting in millions around the world having "A-ha!" moments that led them to create positive change in their lives, which is always a good thing.

Having studied with Brené in graduate school in 2012, it was a lightbulb moment for me when she described the difference between sympathy and empathy using a really easy to understand example (roughly paraphrased here, as I remember it):

Sympathy is like seeing a friend stuck in a deep hole with no way out, looking down at them and saying, "I'm so sorry," while staying safe where you are. You can feel genuine care and concern for them, but they (or their situation) remains solidly outside of your own... by choice.

Empathy is like seeing a friend in that same hole, finding a ladder to climb down to them (while also ensuring that the ladder is there as a way out for you), sitting down beside them in their situation and simply saying, "I'm sorry... and I get it," while giving them the space and time they need to process whatever it is they're going through (i.e. not forcing them to stand up and get out of the hole).

> *"Empathy is seeing with the eyes of another,*
> *listening with the ears of another, and*
> *feeling with the heart of another."*
>
> — Alfred Adler —

In other words, empathy involves relating. Refer back to the segment on perspective: Without the ability to take perspective (either through direct experience or honed skill), empathy is much harder to achieve. In Brené's scenario, a key piece is knowing that you can get back out of the hole, even if your friend doesn't want to. It's a crucial element of empathy, actually. Being able to relate does not mean being emotionally taken down.

That's not relating, and that's not empathy.

That moment in class was a personal "A-ha!" for me. I had never been able to easily explain the difference between the two until that day, even though I knew there was one, since I had experienced it when my father had his stroke a few years earlier.

Of all the people that came to the hospital to visit us, one person stood out in his response. Unlike everyone else who came and offered their condolences and thoughts, which was lovely, this friend of my sister's showed up, put his hands on my shoulders and said, "This sucks." He got it.

In that single moment, I felt seen, understood, and supported. That's empathy.

When it comes to compassion, you need to understand the difference so that you can make a choice on how to act. It's not helpful to anyone if, for example, you would become emotionally undone by being empathetic. In that instance, you might choose sympathy over empathy as part of your expression of compassion. If however, you feel the need to sit with someone in their despair, knowing that you can step away and be okay, then empathy might be your preferred expression of compassion.

What's true is that most compassion requires either empathy or sympathy, which means it requires you to show up. How you choose to show up is up to you. To better understand this, let's describe a different, yet tangible, scenario:

Compassion with empathy might look like working in a soup kitchen and sitting with the clients to talk with them as they enjoy a warm meal, while **compassion with sympathy** might look like sending supplies or resources to the soup kitchen or helping with administrative duties.

Both are examples of compassion in action, and both are helpful to the Receiver. Additionally, both mean you are a Giver. One is not better than the other.

When it comes to compassion, what matters is that you are doing what you are capable of doing so that you can continue to be a Giver.

"Compassion is not a virtue—it is a commitment. It's not something we have or don't have—it's something we choose to practice."

— Brené Brown —

> *"My mission in life is not merely to survive, but to thrive; and to do so with some passion, some compassion, some humor, and some style."*
>
> — Maya Angelou —

Who Do We See As Compassionate?

There are obvious people that we typically label as "compassionate." This often includes: caregivers, helping professionals, fundraisers and philanthropists, and volunteers, to name a few. In their various roles, they are often responsible for the well-being of another person or group.

Many in this group who take on the role through their profession see it as a vocation or calling. While others, such as volunteers, find a sense of purpose in showing up and helping out. This reinforces the notion of humans being hardwired to be part of something and to connect with others.

But who else regularly displays compassion and why (or how) do we come to label their behavior as compassionate? Firstly, let's look at some of the qualities of being compassionate.

They can include being:

- Kind

- Engaged or invested

- Thoughtful

- Helpful

- Emotionally intelligent

- Resourceful (more on this in a moment)

This list is not exhaustive and you can add your own words based on your experience. In fact, it would be a good idea for you to know what your list looks like. So, please go ahead and make one.

The first five items on the list are probably obvious, but it's the 6th item that we need to take a moment to address. Resourcefulness is a common attribute of compassionate people. This means that they have the ability to bring certain things to any situation. In the sympathy/empathy example we used earlier, the resourcefulness included a ladder to be able to climb out of the hole (alone, if necessary).

Resourcefulness, therefore, is more than just financial, though many primarily think of it in that way. But resourcefulness is about all the things you have that can help, which can include: Experience, Connections, Emotional Tools (calm, humor, vulnerability), and Time.

Another attribute that can help us shift who we see as compassionate is: Presence.

There are some individuals that are simply naturally compassionate through the presence they bring to any situation. We know it when we see it. It transcends basic caring and kindness; it's something more. Interestingly, young children often have this level of compassion before they learn otherwise. Their world of constant learning and growing naturally requires them to be present almost all the time. They bring intense focus to almost everything they do.

Think of the last time you watched a 2-year-old stare at a butterfly.

> *"Those who are truly strong can afford to show compassion."*
>
> — Patrik Baboumian —

It's highly likely that they want nothing more than to connect with the butterfly as they watch it in awe. They don't want to kill it, control it, or otherwise impose on it; they want to relate to it, hold it, touch it. They want to understand it. The presence they bring allows them to feel compassion for another living thing.

Of course, this is temporary, as something else will inevitably excite their attention, but for that moment, the attention they are giving an insect can be viewed as compassionate.

They can also do this with humans, especially other children. There are numerous videos online that show interviews with toddlers and pre-schoolers naturally moving to hug another who is sad, or holding hands when someone seems scared. Of course, it's not all children, and of course situations can change this behavior, but in general, if you allow a child to be a child, many will display compassion naturally.

Why? Because at the end of the day, it is in our nature for all humans to be compassionate. All of us.

Unfortunately, by the time we are adults, many of us have been taught that compassion is a form of weakness or detrimental to our situation. A continual message of lack has created a situation where we fear losing out if we share our resources, whatever they may be. This virus of an idea that life is limited in this way has meant that we have lost much of the one thing that makes life more worthwhile: Connection.

Compassion will always result in more connection, not less. When we see a compassionate person, there's a part of us that remembers that... and probably longs for more of it. So, when we ask who do we see as compassionate, we ought to add a second question: Do you see yourself as compassionate?

How Can We Learn Compassion?

"Compassion is the keen awareness of the interdependence of all things.

— Thomas Merton —

As we just discussed, compassion is natural for most people. But, somewhere along the way, it has probably been set aside for other pursuits. What has suffered as a result is multi-layered and includes everything from the planet down to us as individuals. It may seem subtle, but the decline in compassion is anything but small and nuanced... once you add the element of time. So, let's back up for a second.

If we look at indigenous cultures around the world, it wouldn't be a stretch to say that most live in compassionate coexistence with their environment. They use what they need and not more. Their society is not based on consumption, it's based on balance. They know that if they exhaust their resources, they, themselves, will eventually suffer. Of course, there are modern exceptions to this, but in general, it's been their truth for millennia.

It was also the truth for many non-indigenous cultures and peoples around the world up until the industrial revolution and beyond. Though there are still communities who practice subsistence living today (and more are starting to embrace this way of life), in general, consumption is how many of us live. We consume more than we need, because we live in a space of chronic desire. We live in aspiration. There are many reasons for this, but that could be an entire book unto itself. Suffice to say that aspirational messaging (and the promises it offers but rarely keeps) has resulted in societies around the world burning through resources at unprecedented levels. This has led to disconnection from the planet and each other. In short, we are living less compassionate lives in less compassionate societies.

"Compassion. It's not just a word. It's a way of being. It's not just a concept. It's love in action."

— Jeff Brown —

But all is not lost. We can learn compassion. Or, perhaps better stated, we can remember compassion. We can actively pursue a life with more connection, balance, and inner joy and peace. Because compassion has all that to offer, and more. So, how do we do it?

If you feel that you are compassionate already, but would like to increase it, this is for you. If you feel you aren't as compassionate as you would like, this is for you. If you fear you aren't compassionate or have forgotten how to be, this is for you. Even if you know you are compassionate, this is for you. Everyone can benefit from being more compassionate. Here's how to go about it:

- **Focus** — Identify something or someone that you can relate to. This can be a program, a person, an organization, an environment, or almost anything else. The key here is that you can relate to it/them on some level. For example, if you lost a parent to cancer when you were very young, you might identify children in similar circumstances as a group you'd like to connect with and help.

- **Assess** — Identify what needs this person or group might have that are missing or diminished, then identify what resources you have that might help to fill that gap. Be realistic. You cannot give more than you have, nor can you give all that you have. If you deplete yourself it's of no benefit to anyone.

- **Connect** — Find the necessary routes for connection. Look for online groups or local organizations. If you want to support a community, look for opportunities that are group-oriented. If you want to support an individual, look for sponsor-sponsee or mentoring relationship opportunities.

- **Engage** — Make your plan to get involved and do it. This should include understanding what level of commitment you can make. Take that step into compassion and connection.

> "I learned compassion from being discriminated against. Everything bad that's ever happened to me has taught me compassion."
>
> — Ellen DeGeneres —

This acronym (FACE) is deliberate, because ultimately what you're doing is facing your own humanity. Your desire to (re)learn compassion is about becoming more human, more connected, and part of a solution to many of the chronic issues we face in the world. When you take the time to look in the mirror and ask yourself what you can do, you are laying the first stone in the path back to who you are at your core as a naturally compassionate living being.

The short version of all this is: Compassion is remembered through action. While you can teach people to be kind, thoughtful, or caring, compassion is something more. It's a state of being and something we all have access to—we just have to wake it up! Taking action is the best (and possibly only) way to get back to being compassionate. The even better news is that it's self-reinforcing. Once you engage with being compassionate, you remember how it feels and you want to keep that feeling going.

Just remember that compassion doesn't exist solely in big gestures. It can be a hug at the end of a long day or rescuing a bee from almost drowning in a water bucket. It can be as simple as giving a bottle of water to an unhoused person or volunteering to mentor a child who is struggling in school. It can be many different things in a day; in fact, once you start engaging with life this way, it probably will be. The opportunities are almost infinite.

"Compassion for others begins with kindness to ourselves."

— Pema Chödrön —

Once you've started engaging with compassion on a regular basis, you might wonder what it's really doing. You likely already feel better being more compassionate and you know that it's helping others, as well. But what other ripples can it have?

We have discussed many of the effects being more compassionate can create, including the impact it can have on communities, societies, and environments. What we haven't discussed is how being more compassionate—that is, engaging in compassionate behaviors—can impact your inner world. In this scenario, "inner world" refers to both your personal, core relationships with others, and your internal psyche and body.

For your core relationships, there are some very specific benefits. When you are more compassionate, you have more patience and possibly more tolerance. This does not mean that you are a doormat allowing others to walk all over you; you still need to have strong boundaries. It just means that your reactivity is decreased. You are less likely to be reactive when you practice compassion in your relationships.

An example of this may look like being tired at the end of the day and wanting to sit quietly while reading or watching a program on TV while the person next to you (a child, partner, roommate/friend) needs to share a story. Their day was eventful and they are trying to process what happened through sharing. If you can take perspective and see that their need is 1) urgent, and 2) temporary, you might choose to delay your quiet time in order to show up for them. Keeping boundaries, you could say, "I see you need to talk about this. How about we pause the movie for a bit so you can share, and then we can both watch it, together?"

There are many ways you can practice compassion in your relationships while maintaining boundaries. One of my favorite ways to do this is to simply ask: "What do you need from me at this moment?" I then get to assess whether or not I can meet their need once they've stated it. If I can, I will (with boundaries); if I can't, I will suggest something else within my resources.

These types of exchanges often lead to stronger and healthier relationships, which is a wonderful benefit to practicing more compassion in your inner world. But there's another benefit that happens more internally and it's one that fuels itself, seemingly forever.

Being compassionate can create a cyclical cause-and-effect loop in your entire being. In other words, each compassionate action leads to a desire to make another compassionate action. The feel-good chemicals that permeate your body can't help but invite you to do more.

Compassion, therefore, may be addictive, but in the best possible way. And while you may first be engaging in compassionate behavior because it makes you feel better, you will soon come to find that it's easier than not engaging in compassion.

It's easier to be kind, thoughtful, and caring than it is to be cruel, hurtful, and disparaging. The latter are low-frequency emotions, which means they need to continuously be re-upped or reinforced in order to be maintained. They take effort, and ultimately, if they don't take effort, it's because you may have transformed your natural state of being into one that is aligned with fear and hatred. Yikes!

If you want to create a better life for yourself and for others, the way forward is through compassion.

If you want to feel better, the best remedy is compassion. If you want to make the world a better place, it starts with compassion.

A Story About Self-Reinforcing Compassion

Years ago, I met an environmentalist who is passionate about the bug world—something I was not. Though, before I met him, I had spent more than one afternoon watching "bugs" as they went about their daily life. Specifically, I found I could watch ants for hours go in and out of their ant holes with food and other items. Selfishly, I found it to be very meditative; I certainly wasn't doing it for their well-being.

However, I noticed that as I watched the ants, I started to take perspective. I asked myself what the ants must think of me. I am a giant in their world, but am I a threat? Perhaps. I didn't know. Just asking questions, though, was enough to get me to start thinking with more compassion. Fast forward to my meeting the environmentalist.

Through our conversations and connection, I found myself intrigued by his passion for this subset of species that we, as humans, have a tendency to kill any chance we can get. While I have no intention of holding millipedes in my hand, I have started "rescuing" spiders from my home and transferring them outside. I tell myself (and them) that there's no food source for them inside, so they'd do much better outside. I wouldn't have done this years ago, but now I feel good every time I make this decision, knowing that I'm choosing to live in harmony with other creatures, to the best of my ability.

By taking perspective and making connections, I have tapped into compassion for another living being that previously scared me. This is the life-giving power of compassion.

What If I'm Struggling?

"Depression taught me the importance of compassion and hard work, and that you can overcome enormous obstacles. "

— Rob Delaney —

To struggle is part of the human condition. In my experience, there is not a single person on the planet that hasn't experienced some level of struggle. The difference from one person to another resides in the aspects and intensity of the struggle.

For example, some may struggle with mental health while being physically healthy and strong. Someone else may struggle financially, while having great mental health. The variety of struggles humans can experience sometimes feels like a never-ending list.

In short, everyone struggles.

At some point in your life, if you are struggling, you may find yourself feeling resentful and think: "But, who's helping me?" This is especially true if someone suggests you be compassionate toward others while undergoing your own struggles. This is normal.

When we are struggling with something, we are often living in the flight-fight-freeze mode housed in our "reptilian" brain—the part of the brain associated with basic survival instincts.

This means it can be incredibly hard to access the places in our brains that invite connection, such as compassion. So, what do we do?

When this occurs, it's time to go back to basics. If you are struggling, you probably need compassion from others. In the same way that the compassion we practice creates connection for us, we can use connection to receive compassion. Therefore, when we are struggling, the single-most important thing we can do is choose connection. Unless it's a physical/health-related issue that requires some sort of specific intervention, almost all other types of struggle will be improved or lessened by engaging in connection.

This is why process groups (like grief groups or AA) can be incredibly helpful. It's also why finding and creating various points of connection throughout your life is important. If you are already connected, your group will probably see you struggling and reach out to engage with you before you are able to take action yourself.

This type of connection used to be natural, eons ago when we lived in small, tribal communities. The tribe knew that healthy individuals meant a healthy community. They knew that everyone in the group needed to be supported, and not through mandates or obedience, but through compassion and connection.

Therefore, when you're doing well, it's even more important to be compassionate, because compassion creates connection. And when you're struggling, that connection can result in receiving compassion.

Why Do We Need Compassion?

"Everyone deserves compassion."

— Michael Sheen —

There are so many reasons we have already discussed as to why we need compassion. From our basic well-being to the health of the planet as a whole, compassion can make everything better for everyone. It's the ultimate "rising tide" example. A rising tide lifts all boats. The tide doesn't judge or choose, it simply does what it's meant to do as it rises and falls. It doesn't deem one boat more or less worthy than another. It simply shows up and makes sailing possible for every boat in the water.

Compassion does the same thing. Having a more compassionate society can lead to a more balanced (presumably better) world. The ancient Greek philosophers discussed this over 2,000 years ago with both Aristotle (384 – 322 B.C.E.) and Epicurus (341 – 270 B.C.E.) offering helpful perspectives on the subject:

Aristotle – Though he didn't use the word "compassion" directly, he suggested that compassion and indignation are two opposing reactions to imbalance; one to undeserved suffering and the other to undeserved good fortune.

Epicurus – With his focus on the great importance of friendship, he believed that acting with compassion brought forth the greatest pleasure in these relationships.

If we are to take these two perspectives to heart, the core of compassion resides in action, both proactive and reactive. If it is not action to relieve suffering (reactive), it is action taken to increase connection (proactive). When both are practiced, life cannot help but be improved.

"We rise by lifting others."

— Robert Ingersoll —

As if to help us on our way to living with more compassion, we can break these approaches down even further by addressing when we need to practice compassion the most:

- Daily
- In crisis

In our daily lives, practicing compassion with one another and via our special interests (like volunteering) is healthy. It leads to a better state of mental and emotional well-being. It's a proactive, maintenance approach to compassion that brings multiple benefits both to us and to our communities. It's like toppings on a sundae; it just makes everything a little sweeter.

When we are in crisis, however, compassion is a must. It's not the toppings or the ice cream, it's the bowl. Without compassion, very little can happen without potentially causing more mess. When we are in crisis, we need compassion like we need air or water.

Ultimately, we may need compassion from ourselves, but to get through the crisis, we most likely need it from others first. Their compassion gives us the support and understanding we need to create mental-emotional (and sometimes physical) space.

> *"As the human race, let's continue to show love, compassion, and respect towards one another."*
>
> — Amber Liu —

Crises take up an inordinate amount of space in our minds when we are going through them. Having someone help relieve some of the burden can make all the difference.

Similarly, when someone else is in crisis, we get to draw on our resources and offer compassion, especially if we are practicing compassion on a daily basis. This can be a life-affirming response both for them and for us. Compassion can also be easier to offer when we are practicing it regularly.

When we practice compassion in our everyday life, we become more compassionate. When we are more compassionate, we give more compassion to others. It really is that simple.

If you want to live a better life, compassion needs to be part of the equation. More compassion leads to a healthier, more balanced, happier, well-lived life... a life you can look back on with joy, gratitude, and peace.

Conclusion

Practiced in both words and actions, compassion means to:

- Speak kindly with respect, patience, and candor.

- Act thoughtfully with consideration, caring, and acceptance.

Compassion is a healthy undertaking that leads to multiple benefits with no negative side effects (if you remember to have boundaries). Anyone and everyone can benefit from more compassion. It is said that human beings have only exercised a small fraction of their potential.

When you choose compassion as part of your life, you are aligning with the true potential of both the planet and being human.

Compassion is not weakness, nor is it a path to accepting bad (or self-detrimental) behavior. Instead, think of compassion as a superpower—one that means you are more evolved emotionally and ready for what's to come. Being compassionate means that you recognize that you are a part of something greater, whether you consider that to be your community, society, or even the earth and all her species, as a whole.

To be compassionate takes inner strength. It takes clarity of mind and purpose. It takes a belief in something "more" and knowing that together we can help to create that "more"—whatever that may be. It honors the truth that we are all connected and creates a pathway for connection.

> *"The quality of your life is based on the choices you make."*
>
> — Martina E. Faulkner —

About the Author

Martina E. Faulkner is a cross-genre author whose work focuses primarily on exploring what it means to be human, both the unique and the universal. She holds a trifecta in the mental health/healing world as a therapist, certified life coach, and Reiki Master Teacher. This distinctive background allows her to draw on her professional and personal experience in her writing, whether fiction, nonfiction, or poetry.

A self-proclaimed Anglophile, Martina drinks tea daily, loves walks in nature, and enjoys looking at beautiful images from the British Isles while dreaming up her next book. You can read her regular column ('Unique and Universal') on Substack, follow her on Instagram and Facebook @martinaefaulkner, or visit martinaefaulkner.com.

As a children's author Martina's debut children's book, <u>When the World Went Quiet</u>, was given as a gift to Sir David Attenborough, who referred to it as "charming."

Other Books

Understanding Energy
Understanding Resilience
Understanding Gratitude
Understanding Grief
Understanding Karma
50 and F*ck It!
What if..?
Love and Pain
Infinite In My Heart
Me: 365
The Author's Journey
Crafting the Perfect College Essay

Children's Books

When the World Went Quiet
Princess Wigglebottom and the Forgotten Christmas

www.ingramcontent.com/pod-product-compliance
Lightning Source LLC
Chambersburg PA
CBHW041436120626
46547CB00002B/240